CALIFORNIA DYE PLANTS

Californians have long needed an inexpensive natural dye manual with information about Western dye plants and dye methods.

Most natural dye recipes are of eastern United States or European origin, and while some of the recipes can be used with similar plants found in the West, many are not applicable. This discovery led Marilyn Wilkins, a weaving and fiber teacher for Shasta Community College, California, to five years of experimentation with the principles involved using native and common plants for dye colors.

This book contains over 30 recipes for California plants with accompanying plant illustrations by the author, and information about elevations, seasons, and handling for storage.

California
Dye Plants

Marilyn Wilkins

THRESH PUBLICATIONS

Printed in the United States of America

Thresh Publications
441-443 Sebastopol Avenue
Santa Rosa, CA 95401

Library of Congress Cataloging in Publication Data

Wilkins, Marilyn, 1926—
    California dye plants.

    Bibliography: p. 44
    1. Dyes and dyeing, Domestic.   2. Dye plants —
California.   I. Title.
TT854.3.W54   667'.26'09794   76-6172
ISBN 0-913664-08-1

Foreword

During a recent conversation with a friend who teaches Indian culture at one of our state universities and whose tribesmen look to him for leadership and guidance, the purpose of this work was questioned.

We were discussing color plants and his efforts to have the state designate certain Indian plant gathering sites as preserves because of their traditional excellence and use throughout centuries. After painful recounting of highway construction now covering one such site, he went on to point out the uselessness of such a work as this study on dyes from California plants. His position is valid. The plant is a living thing . . . a life. The harmony that an Indian achieves with nature comes about through prayer and regard for the life and spirit that is shared by the plant with man. My friend felt strongly that the recipes would lead to further slaughter and misuse and should be kept to be shared only with care.

However, if these recipes can help us to *see* the native plants and to look with expectancy and pleasure at the prospect of knowing them and all their total character; if we can realize their infinite surprise and delight, sturdiness and fragility; if we can be led to dedicated appreciation and deepest trust, then hopefully my friend could perhaps agree that this work, too, is valid.

Marilyn Wilkins, 1975

Contents

Introduction

The information presented here is intended for use as a supplement to the many fine books now available (at last!) to the home dyer. For a list of these, please note the bibliography. Most other dye recipes are necessarily of Eastern United States or European origin since the practice of home dyeing petered out after coal-tar dyes became known in the late 1850's. Some of these recipes can be successfully applied to similar plants found in the West, but some are not applicable at all, even when the plant is the very same plant. It was this amazing discovery which led me to experiment and finally to try sharing with others some of the information and, more importantly, principles involved in trying to use our native and common plant materials for color.

Any home dyer can tell tales of disgust, heartbreak, and frustration. Any persistent home dyer can tell you dyeing is an infectious disease leading to all sorts of eye-opening, mind boggling experiences. It is a very exciting window from which to see the world around. A dedicated dyer, undaunted by the obnoxious fact that yellow and tan are ubiquitous, casts a covetous eye at every twig and blossom while wondering, would it or wouldn't it? Such a person gradually resolves the obstacles in finding out. Some of these obstacles deserve discussion.

Water in California varies beyond belief. Whatever your water contains will affect your dyeing of wool. However, the most important consideration is that the water be soft. I know people in San Diego, where the Colorado River water is notoriously uncooperative, who use only distilled water purchased commercially; certainly a limiting obstacle. Elevations and locations affect many of our plant dyeing qualities. The recipes here will indicate elevations where important and you should always include it as a notation in your own listings. The seasons are obstacles for the dyer. Most books on the subject make generalizations about picking leaves before the frost, bark in the spring, blossoms when just mature, etc. Also important to the observant home dyer is such information as wet winter, early fall frost, late rains or early rains. Certain plants you want to use or that appear as a surprise are due to just such events. A dyer must learn to take advantage and to anticipate. Dirt is another small, but in some locales, real problem. Some California dirt dyes. Be sure your dye material is carefully rinsed free of foreign matter, especially dirt, before constituting a vat of it. "Keeping" qualities should be of more than general interest to the home dyer. Usually it is best to process (how can you wait to know?) right away, but some of the old Indian methods out here reveal that color is better, and sometimes only available, after the material is dried or fermented.

Admonitions to home dyers in California must necessarily discuss the fact that in many cases our native plants are jeopardized by heavy land use and over-population. Some plants are nearly extinct or are reduced from abundance to protected little treasures.* The lore to be captured before it is lost belongs partly to the dyer, but it is a lore of trust. Therefore, be prepared often to settle for little samples rather than boxes or grocery bags full of rare plants or blossoms required to make up the pound a recipe may require. Some "natives" can be cultivated for dye purposes. This is to be encouraged for two reasons: (1) To reduce the destruction noted above, and (2) to have consistent material. For example, lupine may or may not produce abundantly in the wild, depending on what kind of winter/spring preceded blossom time.

*Note: California Penal Code section 384a makes it a misdemeanor to pick plants and shrubs in public or private places without a permit. (see complete section, page 45)

Wool has special considerations for the dyer. The structure of a wool fiber has three cell forms and it looks something like this under a microscope.

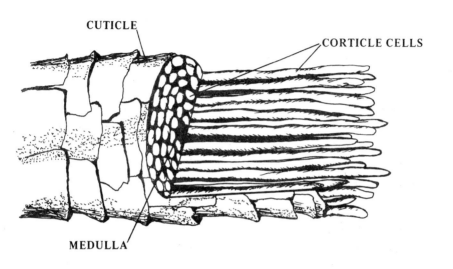

CUTICLE

CORTICLE CELLS

MEDULLA

The scales, the grease which covers the fiber (lanolin), and the complex cell structure are the things which must be kept carefully in mind at each stage of handling the wool. The first, scales, open and close with changes of temperature and they cause wool to mat, or felt, when it is agitated in the washing process. The scales are also what make wool one of the most delightful fibers to spin and work with generally. The grease must be removed before wool fiber will take dye. After careful washing and rinsing of the wool, the home dyer usually can achieve satisfactory results by scouring the wool, i.e., soapy water to cover, brought to a boil, and then simmered for an hour. The grease in wool works *against* you, the dyer, and *for* the life of the wool and its water repellent qualities.

The cellular form and the chemical composition of fibers determine the choice of a mordant. Dyeing wool is a chemical process and in the use of native dyes one sometimes can find a substance which can be used without a mordant. This primary affinity can occur because the native material contains a chemical which will cause both absorption and fixing. I have found, however, that the traditional native dyes, such as green lichen, are of much longer duration and are more light-fast when used with alum mordanted wool.

Procedures for native plant materials and home dyeing can be simple. Some reasons simplicity is possible for me may be helpful for you. I always keep a supply of washed, scoured, alum mordanted, carded wool on hand. I also keep a supply of wool only washed, scoured, and carded. I have a box containing every mordant, measuring spoons, measuring cups, tongs, dowels, glass rod, Glauber Salts, cream of tarter, wool soap, and Calgon water softener. Next to this is a large white enamel kettle, a small enamel kettle, and I use my glass double boiler and enamel lined tea kettle. Enamel gets chips which disturbs dyeing so you must check it before using. I did use an enamel roaster pan of the blue speckled variety until after several disappointing vats I discovered that some process had etched a ring into the enamel all the way around. The reason I keep a sack of alum mordanted wool on hand is that very often you find yourself with a pocket full of a promising piece of moss or leaves or the like. If a snatch of wool is handy all you need is time to process the substance and then wet the wool and add it to the brew. Go from there! *

*Keep all dye materials and chemicals out of children's reach.

Basic Dyeing Process

Most recipes for dyeing wool use measurements of one pound of dry wool to four gallons of liquid dye bath. Deviations are proportionate to these measurements. Containers for dye stuff should be enamel or glass to insure against pollution of the dye bath from the container.

After weighing clean, dry wool (skeins, fleece or cloth), wet it thoroughly by immersing it in soft water and squeezing it — don't stir, agitate or twist it. Add the wool to the dye bath making sure that the vat and wool temperatures are as close as possible.

Bring the vat to boiling point, lower it to simmer and cook the wool gently. Never stir, or agitate it. To test for color or to make additions to the dye vat, be careful to agitate the wool as little as possible.

Remove the wool from the vat, drain it, then lift it carefully to a sink or tub of clear, soft water. The temperature of the rinse water should be as close as possible to the temperature of the dye in the vat. Squeeze the wool, change the water and rinse again — squeezing only. Now the wool can be washed with a mild solution of soapy water, followed by two rinsings. Dry in an airy, shady location.

Exceptions to the basic process are noted in the recipes.

Mordanting

Many of the natural dyes will fade and "bleed" badly unless the yarn or fabric is first treated with a chemical called a mordant, which helps to fix the color to the fiber. The mordants commonly used with natural dyestuffs are alum, chrome (potassium dichromate), copperas (ferrous sulphate), and tannic acid or some other source of tannin such as oak galls.

Wool has the property of holding mordant chemicals in the fibers, and the dyestuff then combines with this mordanted wool to form a permanent color.

ALUM MORDANTING

For each pound of dry wool, use:

4 ounces alum.

1 ounce cream of tartar.

Dissolve the alum and cream of tartar in 4 to 4½ gallons of cold, soft water and immerse the wool yarn or cloth after it has been throughly wet and squeezed out of water. Heat gradually to boiling. Simmer gently for 1 hour. As the water evaporates, add more so that the proportion of liquid to wool remains the same. Cool, and rinse the mordanted material well just before putting it into the dye bath.

Recipes

ACORNS – Color: Orange Tan

Gather acorns early before they get rained on. Break them up, I use kitchen scissors, and cover them with boiling water. They can steep until it's convenient to make your dye bath. Bring them to a boil and simmer the mass until you are sure to have all the color out, about an hour for a pound. Remove the acorns and strain the liquid through a fine sieve as they leave a grainy film in the liquid. White oak acorns give a very nice, lively tan to wool without the use of a mordant.

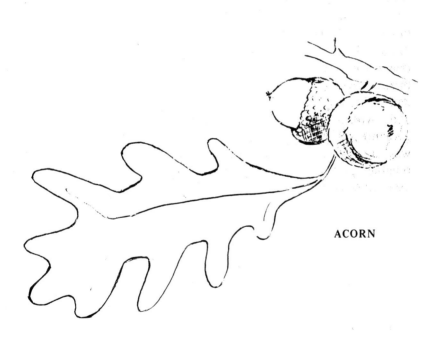

ACORN

ALDER ROOT   Color: Cinnamon

Chop and place in crock, pour boiling water to cover. Put a lid on and let steep a good 24 hours. It can go longer and even ferment! Bring to a boil and simmer about an hour, adding water if necessary. Remove root and dye is ready. Alum mordanted wool yields a soft cinnamon brown. I first saw alder root floating out in a mountain stream. It was a startling, brilliant red. I clipped it and stuffed it in my fishing jacket where it dried. Days later I processed the gray, brown wad it had become, and while it gave no red, it was and is a reliable, pretty color of brown.

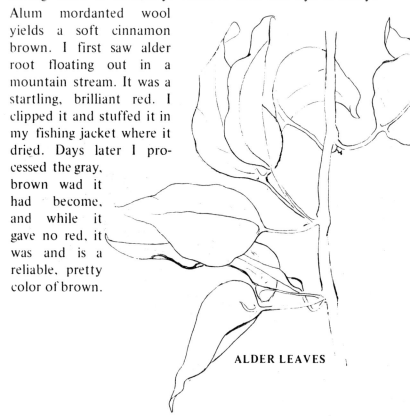

ALDER LEAVES

ALDER BARK   Color: Tan to Brown

Same process as root above.

Alder trees are often to be found fallen down along stream beds. The bark may be used from these dead trees quite satisfactorily.

"AMERICANA" RED TEA ROSE – Color: Green

Folks are always providing me with a plant or bouquet which is certain to end the search for a fine, reliable, red dye. This particular red rose, known and enjoyed in gardens everywhere, yields from its red petals a green that is almost as pretty as the compliment color it comes from.

Pour boiling water over the somewhat bruised petals and simmer until all color is taken from them. You may enjoy your flowers first. They don't have to be used the moment they are picked. Enter wet, alum mordanted wool to the strained vat and simmer about a half hour. Cool in the vat and dry before rinsing.

"AMERICANA" TEA ROSE

ASH TREE LEAVES – Color: Yellow

Ash trees are water loving high altitude trees sometimes confused with alder. Their uniform shape and striking yellow color make them easy to identify. The long pods which are abundant in some years yield an uninteresting tan but the leaves give a beautiful, rich yellow, not quite maize.

Make the vat from green leaves picked just before they turn. They will almost brush off in your hand. Cut them up a little and cover them with boiling water and allow to steep. This can be for a day or two if necessary. Bring to a boil and simmer for an hour until a rich bronze liquid shows. This is the dye vat. Remove leaves, add alum mordanted, wet wool and simmer about an hour. Wool should be very yellow.

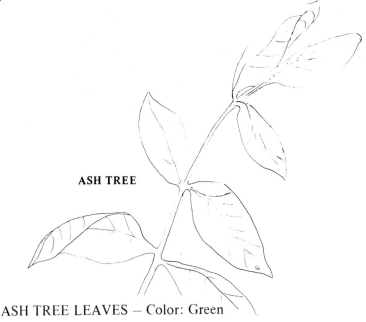

ASH TREE

ASH TREE LEAVES – Color: Green

Make the vat as above. The mordant used is Cu_2SO_4, copper sulfate, and the resulting color is a deep olive green.

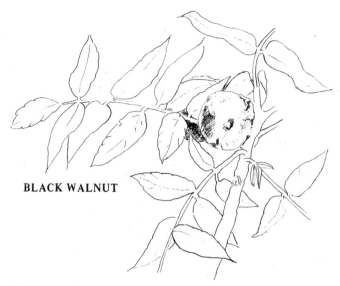

BLACK WALNUT

BLACK WALNUT – Color: Brown

Walnut trees are common throughout California. Most are grafted to Black Walnut roots. If you think there are only English walnut trees in your area, look around. It's worth it to find a source for this rich, brown, satisfying color. You can use just the pulp from hulls outside of the shell or use the whole nut. You won't want to eat the nut afterward! Try to get these while they are just beginning to drop and show a little green. It's disappointing to process a whole gunny sack of nuts, staining your hands and clothes, and end with no color. If the nuts have been rained on or stood long in dewey grass, get them next year. They can be used fresh or dry.

Soak the hulls covered with water for a day or more. Bring to a boil and boil gently for about three hours, adding water to keep the hulls covered. Liquid is now the dye bath.

The old method used no mordant but I use alum and the color is fast. Cooperas may be used for a rich black. Black walnut is interesting to use over black sheep fleeces and over indigo dyed wool. For one pound wool mordanted with alum, use approximately four pounds of hulls. At the last half hour, dissolve 1/2 cup of Glauber Salts and four tablespoons of cream of tartar in water then add to dye.

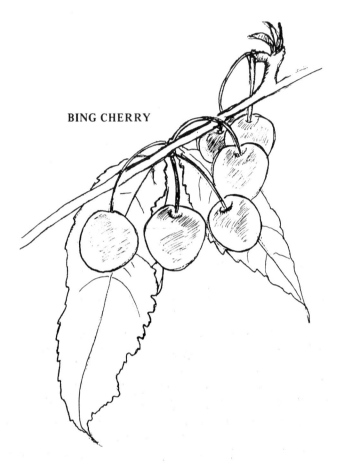

BING CHERRY

BING CHERRY – Color: Purple

Bing cherry trees are not uncommon in the north part of the state. If you have a friend who has one or a place to pick in canning quantity, it can be a good color investment.

Pits and all go into the vat. Cover with boiling water and simmer for an hour adding more water if needed. This is improved if left to stand overnight or even longer. Strain the cherries out and proceed to dye alum mordanted wool. This purple is fast and true.

BRAKEN (Brake) — Color: Brass Yellow

This is the common green fern seen on the floors of California forests and meadows and sought by many in early spring for its succulent new shoots as a tasty green vegetable. It turns golden brown in the fall, but for dye purposes search out healthy, fresh fronds which are fleshy and green. The best vat I ever made from bracken was from an August cutting and which I stored in the refrigerator for six months! I just couldn't cut them when I knew I should in the spring and then I forgot about the vat until the February thaw started my thoughts about spring gathering.

Cut the fronds with scissors into small pieces and place in an enamel kettle. Cover with boiling water and allow to steep at least overnight. Simmer for about an hour, keeping covered with water. Remove refuse and cool.

Place wet, alum mordanted wool into vat and simmer for an hour. Tin may be used at this stage to sharpen the color if desired. Use proportions of one teaspoon tin to three gallons of liquid per pound of wool. Simmer again for no more than a half hour and remove while still warm. Rinse in a soapy bath. Tin can make fibers harsh but it does sharpen and brighten some colors.

BRACKEN

BUCKBRUSH (Ceanothus Cuneatus) — Color: Pink

In the late fall some buckbrush roots are bright pink and red. Chop this root as fine as possible and soak in a crock for at least a week. At the end of this time, place it all in an enamel container and boil for at least an hour or until all color is extracted. Strain out the root. The liquid becomes the dye vat. Enter wet wool and simmer for an hour. No mordant is necessary. An iron kettle may be used to achieve a charcoal pink.

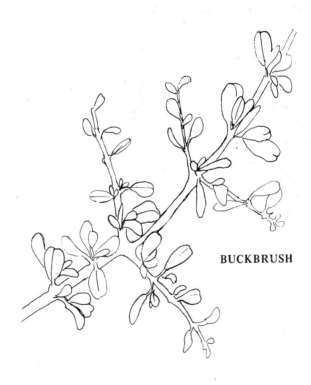

BUCKBRUSH

CAROB PODS — Color: Camel Tan

Carob is a steeet tree found along many of our city residential areas. The pods provide a chocolate substitute commercially, but for the home dyer they are a nice source of a durable camel tan. Gather in the fall and allow to dry. Break into pieces and soak, covered with water for about a week. In an enamel kettle, bring them to a boil in this water and simmer for about two hours or even a half day. Strain the vat and enter wet, alum mordanted wool. Bring to a boil and simmer for an hour. Cool in the vat and dry. Rinse after drying.

CARROT TOPS — Color: Yellow and Green

While not actually a "native", I am including carrot because it does grow everywhere and the tops can be used in every season. The yellow is vibrant and well worth trying for.

Cut tops into pieces and simmer in water to cover for approximately one hour. Remove refuse.

Alum mordanted wool produces a clean yellow.

Blue vitriol, or copper sulfate, used as a mordant, results in a soft olive green. Use in proportions of two ounces of copper sulfate to three gallons of water. This should mordant a pound of wool, scoured and wet. Cool the wool before rinsing.

CEDAR BARK – Color: Cinnamon

Incense Cedar is a tree found in mixed pine forests throughout California from about 2500 feet up to 8500 feet. It has had ups and downs as a commercially valuable timber product. Currently, it is one of the trees left behind when trees are harvested and the dyer can find trees knocked down and accessible for gathering bark. Cedar is easy to identify in a pine forest because instead of a bouquet of needles its greenery is presented in fan-shaped branchlets. The bark is fibrous. Gather strips of it and cut or chop it into a crock to soak covered with water for several days. A rich color will seep out. Transfer it all to an enamel kettle and simmer for an hour. Allow to cool, remove bark. Enter wet, alum mordanted wool and simmer for about a half hour. Tin may be added to sharpen the colors. If used, make a solution in proportions of one teaspoon per three gallons water and one pound wool. Add to the kettle and simmer one half hour or longer.

CONCORD GRAPE – Color: Purple

This old fashioned American native grape provides one of the loveliest purples. For more intense color try to find a supply which is from vines not heavily irrigated.

Gather grapes into an enamel kettle and crush, cover with water and simmer for about an hour, mashing from time to time during the hour. Cool and strain. Enter wet, alum mordanted wool. Simmer about one hour. Tin may be added to sharpen the colors. If used, make a solution in proportions of one teaspoon per three gallons water and one pound wool. Add to kettle and simmer one half hour longer. Cool, dry in the shade and then rinse.

26

DOCK – Color: Light Cinnamon

Western dock, seen along roadsides and in fields as a one- to three-foot brown, seed laden stalk valued for beauty in dry flower arrangements, has a tap root which yields a color hard to duplicate. The root must be dried and then chopped or broken up as small as possible. An Indian recipe advises making it into a paste and putting the yarn and paste away in layers for a few days until all the color seeps into the wool. According to the recipe this should produce orange. However, a light cinnamon brown is the most reliable color I can report.

The broken root is boiled to extract the color and then allowed to soak and even to ferment. Strain the residue for a clean vat and enter wet, alum mordanted wool. Bring to a boil and simmer for about one hour. Cool, dry and rinse.

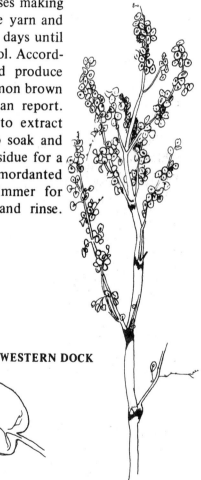

WESTERN DOCK

ELDERBERRY

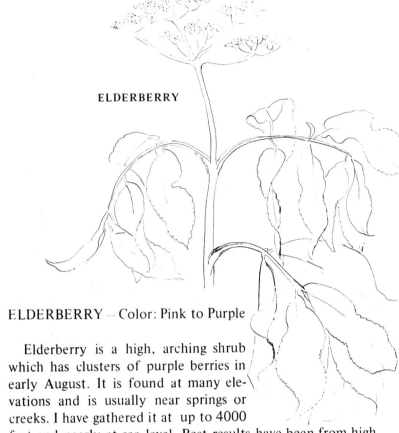

ELDERBERRY — Color: Pink to Purple

Elderberry is a high, arching shrub which has clusters of purple berries in early August. It is found at many elevations and is usually near springs or creeks. I have gathered it at up to 4000 feet and nearly at sea level. Best results have been from high elevation shrubs in full sun and full of juice. The color seems to be light-sensitive. The rich purple color will sometimes change to charcoal black under strong light and it sometimes appears phosphorescent. The pink color from elderberry is quite dull.

Remove most of the stems from the berries and crush the berries in a large enamel container. Bring to a boil and cook until color and juice are extracted. Remove the refuse. At this point you have to resist making jelly! Enter the wet, alum mordanted wool into the juice and simmer one hour. Tin can be added at this stage and simmered for one half hour longer. Remove the wool and while still warm, rinse in a soapy bath.

Tin should be used in proportions of one teaspoon per three gallons liquid.

HORSETAIL — Color: Coral

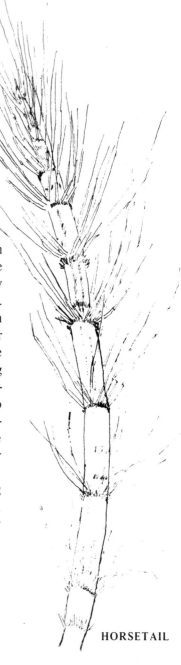

The sturdy, unbranching green stalks of horsetail (equisetum L) are found in marshy places and by streams. There are several varieties. Height varies in location found but in general, the main concern for the dyer is the time of picking rather than the local variety. When found just coming to maturity, early April in the Mendocino coast or May in the Sacramento valley, for example, the color produced is soft coral. If more mature stalks are used, beige or no color results.

Cut the stalks and steep in boiling water to cover at least overnight. Bring to a boil and simmer for an hour or more, keeping covered with water. Let stand again overnight. Remove refuse and enter wet, alum mordanted wool. Simmer for an hour. Cool and allow to steep. Dry, then rinse.

I have never tried it, but I suspect that a chrome mordant here might produce an interesting orange.

HORSETAIL

LAMBS QUARTERS – Color: Beige

This fairly common red-veined weed is also known as pig weed or goosefoot. Sometimes a pest in home gardens, it can be found along roadsides and in old cultivated fields in most of California below 6000 feet from June to October. It is valued as an edible green vegetable, but it also provides a reliable beige dye.

Chop up and boil all parts of the plant and save the liquid for the vat. Use alum mordanted, wet wool and cool in the liquid before rinsing.

LICHEN – Color: Acid Yellow Green

Lichens and mosses are infinite in California. The one used here is the green coarse variety found at 2500 feet or higher and is easy to procure almost all over the state. It can be kept dry until used and it does not require a mordant. Fun for Girl Scouts and vacationers! The deer are apt to eat it off trees up as high as they can reach but you can usually manage a sack full.

Use wool and lichen in equal amount, i.e. pound for pound. Soak the crushed lichen overnight and then boil for an hour. Alum mordanted wool can be used and it does insure color fastness for more years. A greener color can be achieved by adding copper sulfate to the bath after the first cooking. Use proportions of two ounces to three gallons of water and one pound of wool.

LUPINE BLOSSOM — Color: Lime Green

Another state-wide native, lupine grows in many forms and the blossoms vary from yellow to lavender pink. Dye colors from lupine also vary enormously and most are worth the effort involved. This recipe is for "ground" lupine. But bush lupine can be used. The flowers and stems can be cut up together and used, but for clear, exquisite lime green, sit down in a patch of blue ground lupine and carefully slip blossoms from stems around you. Slip only those which have just begun to open or at least have a bud or two left on the stalk. When you move to another spot you'll find it doesn't even show where you have been. Thank goodness! It's a good idea to take a picnic for this is a chore for a sunny spring day. About a quart of blossoms will yield enough color for a half pound of wool. The more quickly they can be processed the better. Place them in the enamel kettle and cover with boiling water. Let steep for a couple of hours then bring to a boil and simmer for one hour. The pretty purple blue vat yields a very lively green color to wet, alum mordanted wool. Blossoms picked as little as two days later will give lime yellow. With copper sulfate added the last half hour a nice olive green results.

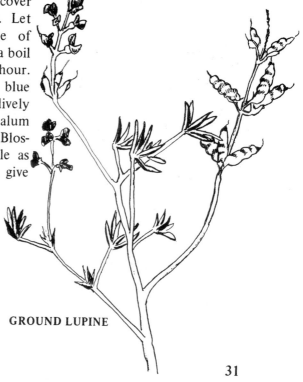

GROUND LUPINE

31

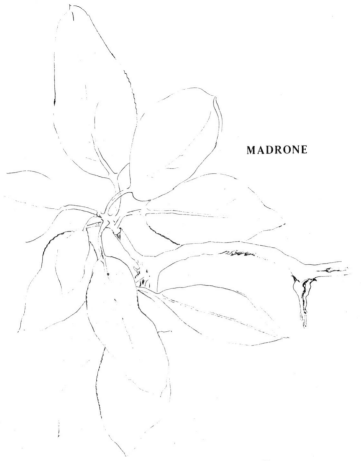

MADRONE

MADRONE TREE — Color: Cinnamon Brown

This handsome evergreen tree found throughout California below 5000 feet is especially abundant in the coast range from San Luis Obispo north. The largest in the world is claimed both in Santa Cruz county and in Trinity county! Although its sweet, beautiful blossoms and handsome berries are distinguishing features, it is the bark which offers interest for the dyer. It shreds off like Eucalyptus bark does and leaves a smooth, shiny surface beneath. Take clean and fresh pieces of the shreds and chop them into an enamel kettle. Soak them covered with water for a week, or even longer. Bring to a boil and simmer for two hours and cool. Strain the vat and enter wet, mordanted wool. Bring to a boil and simmer until the color is well taken. Let cool. Rinse and dry.

MANZANITA – Color: Cinnamon Brown

Manzanita is a common sight in California chaparral and oak-pine forests. Woody and evergreen, its interesting branching is prized when dry. The flakey red bark can be gathered in the fall. Crush and steep in a covered crock for a long time, up to six weeks if you can. Skim off the white film and change to your enamel kettle to boil for a couple of hours. Because it smells like medicine when boiling, I called an Indian friend of mine to find out and sure enough, the bark tea is a cure for colds and sinus. The manzanita apples and leaves are used for other cures.

Strain the residue for a clean vat and enter wet, alum mordanted wool. Bring to a boil and simmer for about one hour for a rich cinnamon brown. Cool, dry, rinse.

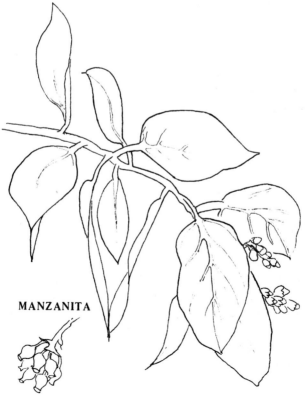

MANZANITA

'MOSS' – Color: Coral Tan

Another very common lichen is the grey-green tufty one which hangs from branches of oak trees and old fruit trees in the woods of California foothills. It can be kept for long periods dried, but the best color results from harvesting in August.

Crush and soak at least overnight. Bring to a boil and simmer, keeping covered with water for about an hour. Let stand to cool, remove by straining for a clean vat. Enter wet, alum mordanted wool and simmer for an hour. Cool or allow to stand overnight in vat before removing the wool and rinsing. I have never seen this color produced synthetically.

MOSS (Grey Rock) – Color: Yellow Tan

This is an abundant moss worthy of gathering. The mosses are hard to describe for identification and it is tempting for this reason to eliminate them altogether. This one is easy to find due to its color and abundance at elevations above 4,000 feet along trails and in campsites. On rocks it stands up in tufts and is easy to gather.

Crush the dry moss and cover with water. Soak overnight and then bring to a boil. Simmer for about an hour. Cool, strain the vat and enter wet alum mordanted. wool. Simmer for about a half hour and allow to cool in the vat. Dry, then rinse.

MULLEIN – Color: Yellow - widely distributed

Flannel plant, common mullein (verbascum thapsus) is not turkey mullein.

This woolly plant stands dramatically tall on vacant lots, roadsides, and in cultivated gardens from early June until frost. It has tall spikes covered with yellow blossoms. Cut just before frost. The whole plant or just clean, select leaves can be used. It can be hung to dry and used later with little damage to color, but no color will result from picking too early. Cut into an enamel kettle and cover with boiling water, steep at least an hour or overnight, bring to a boil and simmer for about an hour. Remove refuse. Enter wet, alum mordanted wool and simmer for an hour.

This plant, so easy to gather and available everywhere yields a true, sunny yellow. It also makes a delicious tea!

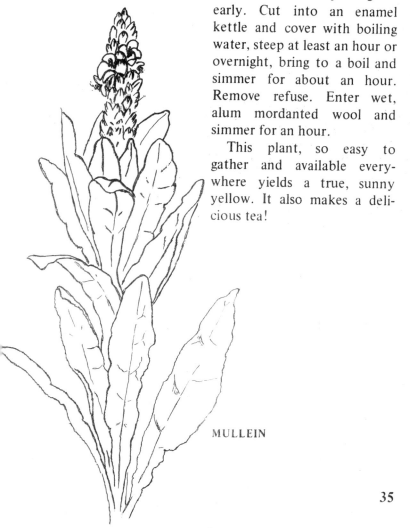

MULLEIN

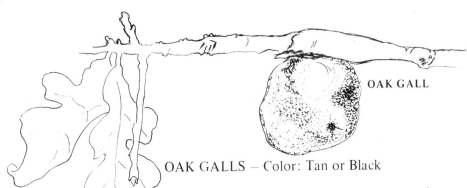

OAK GALL

OAK GALLS — Color: Tan or Black

Oak galls, or balls, are knobby little growths on white and black oak trees. They are sometimes puffy and hollow, making a treat for children to pop, but the ones a dyer will seek are solid. Collected in the fall, they are tan colored. If you cut one open you'll find in the heart a little creature who created the growth. The galls will be dry and hard. Break them and either crush them or whiz them in a blender to make a powder. The natural tannin, valued in early dyeing practices is so concentrated that a mordant isn't necessary for achieving a tan color.

Make a paste with the powder and let it stand overnight. Stir hot water into it, enough to make a vat and bring to a boil. Simmer for a half hour. Cool and allow to steep over-night. Strain the vat and enter wet, natural wool. Bring to a boil and simmer for one half hour.

An iron kettle may be used to produce a charcoal tan effect, or copperas (ferrous sulfate) may be added to the vat to produce a black color. Use proportions of three gallons liquid to three ounces of copperas to one pound of wool.

PEACH LEAVES · Color: Yellow

Peach trees are found nearly everywhere in California. Their leaves yield an arresting, brilliant yellow.

Gather the leaves from the tree just before they begin to turn color in late summer or fall. They will drop easily into your hand if they are at that stage. Fill your enamel container and cover with water. Let stand overnight or longer and then bring to a boil and simmer for an hour. Let stand again, at least to cool, and better for several hours. Remove the leaves and enter wet alum mordanted wool. Simmer for approximately one hour. Some people add tin for the last half hour, but I have never found it necessary.

POPPY - CALIFORNIA POPPY — Color: Yellow

Poppies, golden poppies gleaming in the sun,
Closing up at evening, when the day is done,
Pride of California, Flower of our State,
Growing from the mountains to the Golden Gate!!

Do California school children still learn this song during first school days? Do they still learn that picking that Pride of California is against the law?

Poppies do grow almost everywhere in the state from about 2,000 feet down to sea level and blossom from June to September. Their color varies widely from straw to rich orange. While there are several varieties, it is generally agreed that the poppy is the most highly developed in the interior valleys, although, no matter where you find them it is important to do your picking on private land with the owner's permission. Luckily, like Lupine, poppies are happy in a garden and can be cultivated easily and with reward to the dyer.

The dye process is also similar to Lupine. Snip off the bright heads, place in an enamel or glass container, and pour enough boiling water over them to cover. Steep at least an hour and then raise the temperature to a boil. Simmer for one half hour, turn off the heat and cool. More water may be needed after the first steep to make enough liquid for a bath. Remove the blossoms. Enter wet, alum mordanted wool and simmer for approximately one half hour. The yellow color will vary from light to dark, but is seldom acid in character. Use wool in proportions of one pound to three gallons of liquid vat.

QUEEN ANNE'S LACE

QUEEN ANNE'S LACE or WILD CARROT — Color: Yellow

Lovely Queen Anne's Lace follows the Brodiaea in the wild flower procession through May and June all over California. Find it in open fields and along roadways where it has some moisture for luxuriant growth. It is one of the beauties that can be cultivated easily and that may be because it was a garden flower to begin with. The soft yellow is best brought on by steeping the cut stalks and blossoms in boiling water overnight and then simmering for approximately an hour. Discard refuse. Enter wet, alum mordanted wool. Simmer for a half hour and allow wool to cool in the vat. I prefer to dry the wool unrinsed. Once dried, it can then be rinsed. When color is fragile and harshness of the wool is not a factor, I think the results are better using this procedure.

REDBUD BARK — Color: Rose Tan

The outer bark of the western redbud yields a substantial rose-tan color. I am told that the inner bark yields a color also, but I have never been able to extract it nor have I found any in the roots. An Indian friend of mine remembers the spring chore of gathering gunny sacks full of redbud root, but cannot remember the color! I can't get it by my systems, though some year I do hope to stumble onto the secret.

Strip the bark in spring and cut into small pieces. Pour boiling water over to cover and steep for at least twenty-four hours. Bring to a boil and simmer. Strain through a sieve to obtain a clear vat and enter wet, alum mordanted wool. Simmer for an hour and allow to cool in the vat before rinsing.

REDBUD TWIG

REDBUD LEAVES AND PODS — No Color

I only mention these because the beautiful pink leaves are so impressive it seems they must have color. They do not. Redbud also hangs heavily with spectacular brown pea shaped pods in the fall. These are also disappointing for the dyer.

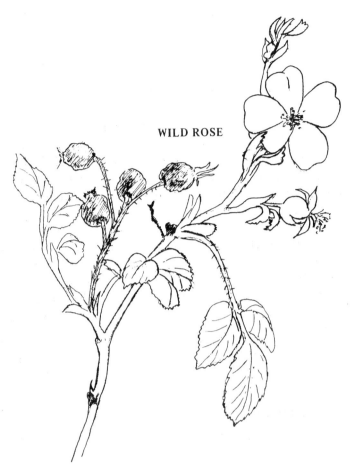

WILD ROSE

ROSE HIPS -- Color: Beige

The California Wild Rose is common everywhere in the state except at high altitudes. In "back country" scenes, thickets are often clues to bottle hunters that an area has remained undisturbed. Blossoms are pink and single and bushes get rank and thick where moisture is adequate. The "hip" is bright red and available after blossom time in late summer and fall. I always gather enough for a supply of tea as well as dye. It's a good source of Vitamin C. The hips can be dried or used fresh.

Crush them slightly and cover with boiling water. Simmer approximately one hour. Strain the vat and enter wet, alum mordanted wool. Simmer wool, dry and rinse.

WILD BUCKWHEAT – Color: Yellow

Not uncommon at elevations from 2,000 to 4,000 feet in August, this lovely bouquet can be found in rocky mountain places and along trails. It has many relatives ranging in colors from white to rose, but the yellow from this is exactly what you see when you gather it, no more or less. It is an earthy, soft yellow.

Cut the button-like blossoms into a glass or enamel container. Cover with boiling water and simmer for approximately an hour. Allow to cool. Remove blossoms. Enter wet, alum mordanted wool and bring to a boil. Simmer about half an hour or until color appears well taken.

WILD GRAPES – Color: Purple

In the coast range, north to the Oregon border and in Sierra foothills in late October and November, one sees flaming red leaves scrambling up tree trunks and sprawling over rocks and sand along streams and in canyons. These are the wild grape vines. The grapes hide under the leaves in blue clusters and are tiny compared to commercial varieties. They make delicious jelly and a pretty, light purple dye if picked when ripe and after a frost. A gray lavender results from picking too early.

WILD GRAPE

The procedure is the same as for Concord Grape.

WILLOW – Color: Red Brown

I hesitate to report dye from willow for the same reason as for moss and lichens. There are so many, many varieties of willow. Pussy willows are not just pussy willows! Most of them yield color that can be made some other way and usually some shade of yellow. However, in the spring mixed in with several varieties, is a willow worth watching for. Looking down a creek bed or marshy canyon in California foothills one can see red twigs casting a pretty glow on the scene. Choose these thin twigs to gather for your color. If picked and

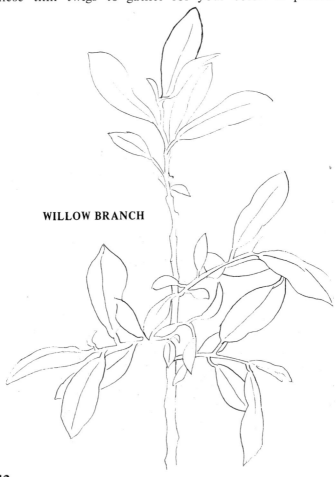

WILLOW BRANCH

stripped just right you could weave them into baskets and the color would stay forever I am told. For dyeing, cut them into pieces and cover with boiling water. Let steep for a day and then make a vat by simmering for an hour or until you have extracted all color possible. Enter wet, alum mordanted wool leaving the twigs in the vat. Cool before rinsing.

YEW BARK — Color: Cinnamon Brown

Use the same procedure as for cedar.

Yew has traditionally been used by California Indians for making bows and paddles. It is found in damp parts of our mixed evergreen forests and at medium-high elevations. The wood is quite heavy and bark slips off in thin, parchment-like strips similar to madrone but coarser and tighter.

Bibliography

Adrosko, Rita J., *Natural Dyes and Home Dyeing.*
American Encyclopedia.
Birrell, Vera., *The Textile Arts.*
Bolton, Eileen., *Lichens for Vegetable Dyeing.*
Brooklyn Botanical Garden Record., *Dye Plants and Dyeing
         – A Handbook.*
Davenport, Elsie G., *Your Yarn Dyeing.*
Davidson, Mary Francis., *The Dye Pot.*
Ferlattle, William J., *A Flora of the Trinity Alps of Northern
         California.*
Furry, Margaret S. and Bess Viemont., *Home Dyeing with
         Natural Dyes.*
Holt, Vera., *Keys for Identification of:*
        Wildflowers
        Ferns
        Shrubs
        *Woody Vines of Northern
         California.*
Jepson, Willis Linn., *A Manual of Flowering Plants of
         California.*
Krochmal, Arnold and Connie., *Complete Illustrated Book of
         Dyes from Natural Sources.*
Lesch, Alma., *Vegetable Dyeing.*
McMinn, Howard E., *Illustrated Manual of California Shrubs.*
Morrow, Mable., *Magic in the Dyepot.*
Munz, Phillip A., *California Flora.*

PENAL CODE SECTION 384a

Trees, shrubs, ferns, etc.; cutting, destroy-
ing or removing from highway
rights-of-way or public or private
lands without permit; punishment;
enforcement; confiscation; exceptions

Every person who within the State of California wilfully or negligently cuts, destroys, mutilates, or removes any tree or shrub, or fern or
herb or bulb or cactus or flower, or huckleberry or redwood greens, or
portion of any tree or shrub, or fern or herb or bulb or cactus or
flower, or huckleberry or redwood greens, growing upon state or
county highway rights-of-way, or who removes leaf mold thereon;
provided, however, that the provisions of this section shall not be
construed to apply to any employee of the state or of any political
subdivision thereof engaged in work upon any state, county or public
road or highway while performing such work under the supervision of
the state or of any political subdivision thereof, and every person who
willfully or negligently cuts, destroys, mutilates or removes any tree or
shrub, or fern or herb or bulb or cactus or flower, or huckleberry or
redwood greens, or portions of any tree or shrub, or fern or herb or
bulb or cactus or flower, or huckleberry or redwood greens, growing
upon public land or upon land not his own, or leaf mold on the surface
of public land, or upon land not his own, without a written permit
from the owner of the land signed by such owner or his authorized
agent, and every person who knowingly sells, offers, or exposes for sale,
or transports for sale, any tree or shrub, or fern or herb or bulb or
cactus or flower, or huckleberry or redwood greens, or portion of any
tree or shrub, or fern or herb or bulb or cactus or flower, or huckleberry or redwood greens, or leaf mold, so cut or removed from state or
county highway rights-of-way, or removed from public land or from
land not owned by the person who cut or removed the same without
the written permit from the owner of the land, signed by such owner
or his authorized agent, shall be guilty of a misdemeanor and upon
conviction thereof shall be punished by a fine of not more than five
hundred dollars ($500) or by imprisonment in a county jail for not
more than six months or by both such fine and imprisonment.

The written permit required under this section shall be signed by
the landowner, or his authorized agent, and acknowledged before a
notary public, or other person authorized by law to take acknowledg-
ments. The permit shall contain the number and species of trees and
amount of shrubs or fern or herbs or bulbs or cacti or flowers, or
huckleberry or redwood greens, or portions of any tree or shrub and
shall contain the legal description of the real property as usually found
in deeds and conveyances of the land on which cutting or removal, or

both, shall take place. One copy of such permit shall be filed in the office of the sheriff of the county in which the land described in the permit is located. The permit shall be filed prior to commencement of cutting of the trees or shrub or fern or herb or bulb or cactus or flower or huckleberry or redwood green or portions of any tree or shrub authorized by the permit. The permit required by this section need not be notarized or filed with the office of the sheriff of the county where trees are to be romoved when 5 (five) or less trees or 5 (five) or less pounds of shrubs or boughs are to be cut or removed.

Any county or state firewarden, or personnel of the California Division of Forestry as designated by the State Forester, and personnel of the United States Forest Service as designated by the Regional Forester, Region 5, of the United States ForestService, or any peace officer of the State of California, shall have the full power to enforce the provisions hereof and to confiscate any and all such shrubs, trees, ferns or herbs or bulbs or cacti or flowers, or huckleberry or redwoood greens or leaf mold, or parts thereof unlawfully cut or removed or knowingly sold, offered or exposed or transported for sale as hereinbefore provided.

The provisions of this section shall not be construed to apply to any tree or shrub, or fern or herb or bulb or cactus or flower, or geeens declared by law to be a public nuisance.

The provisions of this section shall not be deemed to apply to the necessary cutting or trimming of any such trees, shrubs, or ferns or herbs or bulbs or cacti or flowers, or greens if done for the purpose of protecting or maintaining an electric power line or telephone line or other property of a public utility.

The provisions of this section do not apply to persons engaged in logging operations, or in suppressing fires.

Plant illustrations by Marilyn Wilkins. Cover and book design by Christine Romine. Text set in Press Roman 11 point on an IBM Electronic Selectric Composer. Negatives by Byron Rabbitt with a Pos 1 camera. Printed on an A.B. Dick 326 by Robert Thresh on 70 lb white offset book paper. Collated and then bound on a Bindfast II by Sydney Sue Scott.